WILD CANINES!

COYOTE

By Jalma Barrett
Photographs by Larry Allan

BLACKBIRCH PRESS, INC.
WOODBRIDGE, CONNECTICUT

Published by Blackbirch Press, Inc.
260 Amity Road
Woodbridge, CT 06525

Email: staff@blackbirch.com
Web site: www.blackbirch.com

©2000 by Blackbirch Press, Inc.
First Edition

Printed in the United States

10 9 8 7 6 5 4 3 2 1

All photographs ©Larry Allan, except page 17: ©Corel Corporation.

Dedication
For Pamela

–JB and LA

Library of Congress Cataloging-in-Publication Data
Barrett, Jalma.
Coyote / by Jalma Barrett : photographs by Larry Allan.
        p.   cm. — (Wild canines!)
    Includes bibliographical references (p.) and index.
    Summary: Describes the physical appearance, habits, hunting, and mating behaviors, family life, and life cycle of coyotes.
    ISBN 1-56711-261-7
    1. Coyotes—Juvenile literature. [1. Coyotes.] I.Title. II.Allan, Larry, ill.
QL737.C22B34   2000
599.77'25 21—dc21   99-04028
                                                                            CIP

Contents

Introduction

Coyotes are the most numerous of the 7 wild canids (dog-like animals, including wolves and foxes) found in North America. Popular cartoons often show coyotes as "wily," or sly tricksters. That image of the animal is partly true—coyotes are intelligent and highly adaptable (able to change to fit new conditions).

It used to be that coyotes were found only in southern and eastern Alaska, southern and western Canada, and the western United States. But today, as wolves are disappearing from eastern areas of the United States, coyotes are expanding into abandoned wolf habitat.

Where Coyotes Are Most Common

Coyote territory

Coyote habitats have increased during recent years.

Coyotes are now found throughout the United States. In the West, they prefer to live on the open plains. In the East, however, coyotes inhabit brushy areas. They are also found in Mexico and Central America.

Physical Appearance

Coyotes are similar to other North American canids in several ways. All canids have slim bodies; long, pointed muzzles (nose and jaw); triangle-shaped ears; long, slender legs; and bushy tails. There are a few traits that are unique to coyotes. Their ears are larger and more pointed than wolves' ears. Their muzzles are also longer and narrower than wolves' muzzles.

Coyote ears are longer and more pointed than wolf ears.

Coyotes' coats are various shades of gray or beige. Sometimes, they have orange fur mixed into their backs. They are tan or brownish-yellow underneath. Their long legs are yellow or rust-colored, with a dark line on their forelegs. Their bushy tails have black tips.

Most coyotes weigh between 20 and 40 pounds (9–18 kilograms). Some can reach 55 pounds (25 kilograms).

The Tale of the Tail

If you see a dog-like creature running through the woods, you may not know right away if it's a wolf, a coyote, or a dog. There's one sure way to tell the difference: It's all in the tail. A coyote runs with its tail down. A wolf runs with its tail straight out. And a dog runs with its tail pointing up. 🐾

Coyote

Wolf

Dog

Most stand 23 to 26 inches (58–66 centimeters) tall at the shoulder. In comparison, coyotes stand an inch or two taller than Labrador retrievers, but only weigh half as much as those dogs do. Coyote bodies are 3.5 to 4.5 feet (105–132 centimeters) long, with tails from 12 to 15 inches (30–39 centimeters). Desert-dwelling coyotes average about 25 pounds (11 kilograms) and are smaller than their cold-weather relatives. These smaller bodies help coyotes survive in the hot desert because they are easier to keep cool. Larger bodies are better suited for animals in cooler regions because they have more bulk and are easier to keep warm.

Special Features

All wild canines have excellent hearing, sight, and sense of smell. Their keen senses help them locate prey quickly. Like other predators, coyote eyes face forward. This gives them binocular vision, the ability to focus both eyes together on one object. It also gives them depth perception so they can judge the distance to prey. A reflective layer inside their eyes improves night vision. This layer bounces light back, giving the light-sensitive cells (rods) in the eyes a second chance to absorb light.

Coyotes are the fastest of all wild canid runners.

An excellent sense of smell enables coyotes to track their prey.

Coyotes are also among the best wild canine runners. They generally cruise at speeds of 25 to 30 miles (40-50 kilometers) per hour, but can reach speeds of up to 40 miles (65 kilometers) per hour in short bursts.

The most important feature of coyotes is their super adaptability. This feature has made them highly successful in expanding their habitat and increasing their population. In the past, large numbers of wolves, cougars, and bears were hunted by humans. This greatly reduced their populations and allowed coyotes to move into those animals' habitats. The growth of farming—especially in the Midwest—also provided increased rodent populations, a major food source for coyotes.

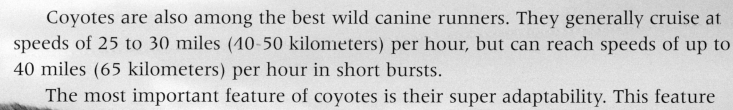

Coyotes are highly adaptable to change, which makes them true survival specialists.

Social Life

Coyote social structure varies—some form wolf-like family groups, and others prefer to live alone. As with wolves, a coyote alpha pair (the strongest male and female) will lead the pack, which usually has from 4 to 8 members.

At dawn, dusk, and during the night, coyotes may let out a series of barks and yelps. Then, they may follow with a long howl, which ends in yips. This vocalization helps members of the family keep track of each other in the dark. One call will usually get an answer right away.

Then others will join in—producing a chorus of howls. Not all howling is for communication. Some coyotes will howl just for the sheer joy of it. Coyotes don't bark as much as domestic dogs. For them, barking without a howl is a threat to other animals, usually in defense of a kill or a den.

Like other canids, coyotes mark their territories. Both urine and feces (droppings) serve as scent markers, which are usually placed on tree trunks or rocks. Raising their markers puts the scent up closer to the nose level of passing animals. Strangely, coyotes often choose the center dividing line on a highway as a highly visible place for their markers.

Opposite: Some coyote howling helps members of a pack or family keep track of each other.
Above right: Coyotes mark their territories with strong scents.
Below right: Some coyotes howl for the sheer joy of it.

Hunting for Food

Coyotes hunt alone, in pairs, or in small family groups. The group hunt begins when the coyotes all yelp in unison. This yelping alerts the members and organizes them. Coyotes are known to eat anything they can chew, and their diets vary widely. In the dry Southwest, for example, coyote diets include rabbits, rats, deer, mice, grasshoppers, juniper berries, cactus fruit, and carrion (already-dead animals). In wetter areas, frogs, toads, hares, gophers, snakes, and various kinds of regional fruit might be added to the coyote diet.

A coyote stalks its prey like a pointer dog—it holds still, watching carefully before it pounces. One observer saw a coyote stay completely still, with one paw up in the air, for more than 11 minutes! For larger prey, like deer, 2 or more coyotes must work together to make the kill. They also take turns chasing jackrabbits or other fast runners, tiring their prey until they can catch it.

Coyotes stalk their prey by sneaking up on a target and then pouncing.
Opposite: Coyotes hunt alone or in small groups.

Coyotes have also been known to team up with other animals. Sometimes, coyotes and badgers will work together. Coyotes have actually been seen herding badgers toward burrows where prey is hiding. Both predators benefit from this unlikely partnership. As a badger burrows after a ground squirrel, for example, a coyote stations itself at an escape hole. If the prey comes out, the coyote grabs it for a meal. This does not always benefit the coyote, however. If the prey senses the coyote's presence, it often stays underground. This gives the badger a better chance of capturing it.

Some coyotes will work together with another animal to trap prey. Working with a badger, a coyote will wait at an escape hole as prey is forced out of its burrow.
Opposite: A lone coyote devours a recently caught squirrel. Small rodents are easy prey for animals hunting alone.

The Mating Game

Coyotes pair off for several years, sometimes even for life. This is called long-term pair bonding. Between February and April, coyotes will begin their cycle of reproduction. Generally, only the alpha pair mates. Beta females (those second in rank in the pack) will breed only if the pack is losing members or if its population is threatened.

Male and female coyotes pair off for long periods of time.

Mother and father coyotes work together to raise their young.

Coyote dens are usually dug along river banks or on dry slopes of canyons or gulches. The female might dig a new den or enlarge an abandoned badger, fox, or ground squirrel burrow. As coyotes dig into the ground, the uplifted soil forms into the shape of a fan or a mound around the entrance. Coyotes may also use dens above ground, settling inside a cave or log.

Coyotes use dens only for raising their pups. The parents usually have several emergency dens in the area, and if the pups are threatened they can be moved to a safer location. The dens are abandoned when the young are old enough to survive on their own.

Coyote Pups

A litter of 1 to 19 pups (usually 5 to 10) is born 63 days after adults mate. The pups are born blind and helpless. Only after 10 or 11 days do their eyes open. The young step out of their den for the first time at about 3 weeks of age. At 4 weeks, pups get their first solid food, which is regurgitated (brought back from the stomach to the mouth) by adults. Last year's offspring will also help parents provide food for the new pups. Although they begin to get teeth at about 6 weeks old, the young will nurse for 12 weeks. When pups are about 3 or 4 months old, parents bring small rodents to the den.

Top: A pup first leaves its den at 3 weeks of age.
Left: A pup's first solid food is pre-chewed and partially digested by the parents.

A young pup peeks out from the safety of its tree trunk den.

Eventually, live prey is brought to the pups so they can learn to catch and kill animals themselves. Coyotes must learn their survival skills. As part of their training, pups will chase blowing leaves, tumbling bits of fur, and other debris. They jump on, and stalk, these items to practice the skills they will need for adult life. Like other wild canids, coyote pups also pounce and jump on each other, snarling and snapping. Later, this helps to establish the social order or dominance (power) ranking within the pack.

In autumn, the pack changes. Beta, or secondary, adults may decide to leave, either to live alone or to form another pack with other individuals. Some pups choose to spend a second year with their parents. By winter, the pack's population is set and the group is ready to begin the life cycle once more.

In the wild, coyotes may live to be 6 to 8 years old. One coyote is known to have lived more than 14 years in the wild. Another reached 18 years in captivity (cared for by humans).

Opposite top: A coyote mother returns to the den with some captured prey for her pups.

Opposite bottom: Pups bite at their mother's mouth to stimulate regurgitation.

Right: Early play establishes the social order among youngsters.

Inset top: Pup's first howl.

Inset bottom: Play stalking and hunting prepare pups for survival on their own.

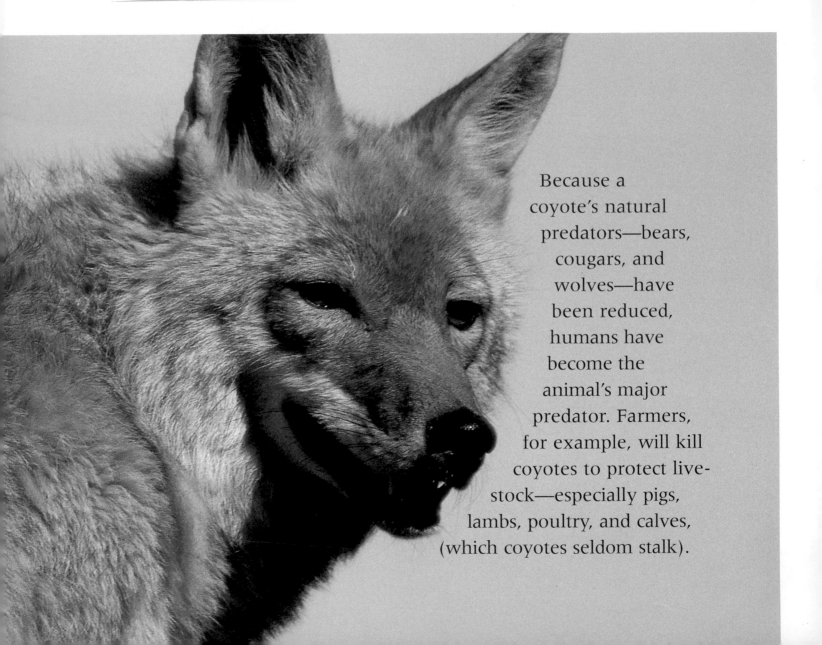

Coyotes and Humans

Because a coyote's natural predators—bears, cougars, and wolves—have been reduced, humans have become the animal's major predator. Farmers, for example, will kill coyotes to protect livestock—especially pigs, lambs, poultry, and calves, (which coyotes seldom stalk).

During the 1970s and 1980s, coyotes were also killed for their pelts (skin of fur-bearing animals). But the fur industry has declined greatly since then, and coyote pelts are of little value today.

Coyotes can live successfully near humans. Despite human efforts to destroy, or at least lessen, the coyote population, these survival specialists have maintained their position in the West, and are increasing their numbers in the East. Many people fear these creatures, or see them as pests. But, coyotes are unique and useful animals that help to maintain the balance of nature. They use their extraordinary hunting and survival skills to capture prey and keep other populations in control.

Coyote Facts

Scientific Name: *Canis latrans*

Shoulder Height: 23" to 26"
(58 to 66 centimeters)

Body Length: 3.5' to 4.5'
(105 to 132 centimeters)

Tail Length: 12" to 15"
(30 to 39 centimeters)

Weight: 20 to 40 pounds
(9 to 18 kilograms)

Color: Gray, beige, tan, and yellow

Sexual Maturity: 1 to 2 years

Gestation: 63 days

Litters Born: 1 per year

Litter Size: 1 to 19 pups

Social Life: Small, highly structured groups; pairs; or solitary

Favorite Food: Opportunistic eaters (anything they can chew)

Range: Continental United States, southern and western Canada, southern and eastern Alaska, Mexico, and Central America

GLOSSARY

adaptability The ability to change in order to fit into a new situation.

habitat The place and natural conditions in which a plant or animal lives.

herding To make animals move together as a group.

predator An animal that lives by hunting other animals.

stalking To hunt in a quiet, secret way; usually in pursuit of prey.

trait A quality or characteristic that makes one thing different from another.

FOR MORE INFORMATION

Books

Lepthien, Emilie. *Coyotes* (A New True Book). Danbury, CT: Children's Press, 1993.

Ryden, Hope. *Your Dog's Wild Cousins*. New York, NY: Lodestar Books, 1994.

Winner, Cherie. *Coyotes* (Nature Watch). Minneapolis, MN: Carolrhoda Books, 1995.

Web Sites

Family Canidae

Learn more about coyotes and their relationship to foxes and wolves—
sciweb.onysd.wednet.edu/sciweb/zoology/mammalia/dog.html.

GeoZoo: Wolves, Coyotes, Foxes & Relatives

Details on each species in the Canid family and how they are related—
www.geobop.com/Mammals/Carnivora/canidae/index.htm.

INDEX